FRESH AS A DAISY

Nature Idioms
(A Multicultural Book)

By Diane Costa

Illustrated by Maria Russo

Language Lizard
Basking Ridge

For English audio and resources for teaching idioms, see the last page of this book.

Fresh as a Daisy
Copyright © 2020 Language Lizard
Published by Language Lizard
Basking Ridge, NJ 07920
info@LanguageLizard.com

Visit us at www.LanguageLizard.com

First edition 2020

Library of Congress Control Number: 2020906440

ISBN: 978-1-951787-08-0 (Print)
ISBN: 978-1-951787-09-7 (Ebook)

WHAT IS AN IDIOM?

An idiom is a phrase that says one thing but means something different. An idiom can be a quick way of saying something complicated. Knowing idioms will help you to understand and speak English fluently. This book contains idioms about nature.

OVER THE MOON

Meaning: To be very excited and happy

She was **over the moon** when she won the street art contest.

PUT DOWN ROOTS

Meaning: To settle down somewhere and stay

After moving almost every year, my family decided to **put down roots** in a big city.

A RAY OF SUNSHINE

Meaning: Something that brings happiness and hope

The baby's smile was **a ray of sunshine** for his mother.

A BREATH OF FRESH AIR

Meaning: A refreshing change

After wearing my school uniform all day, wearing my party dress was **a breath of fresh air**.

UNDER THE WEATHER

Meaning: Feeling unwell

She couldn't go to the festival because she was **under the weather**.

MAKE A MOUNTAIN OUT OF A MOLEHILL

Meaning: To overreact to something small

After getting just one question marked wrong, the student complained and **made a mountain out of a molehill**.

A NEEDLE IN A HAYSTACK

Meaning: Something very difficult to find

Finding her lost *oware* stones was like looking for **a needle in a haystack**.

NIP IT IN THE BUD

Meaning: Stop something when it is just beginning

When the teacher noticed bullying at recess, she **nipped it in the bud**.

DOWN TO EARTH

Meaning: Being practical and realistic

I was surprised that the famous movie star was easy to talk to and **down to earth**.

TIP OF THE ICEBERG

Meaning: A small part of a bigger problem

The messy kitchen was just the **tip of the iceberg**. The rest of the house looked worse.

21

THROUGH THE GRAPEVINE

Meaning: To learn about something through gossip

I heard **through the grapevine** that my neighbors were moving.

STOP AND SMELL THE ROSES

Meaning: To take your time, relax, and enjoy yourself

I was in a hurry to get there, but my grandfather said to **stop and smell the roses**.

CHASING RAINBOWS

Meaning: Trying to achieve something that is unlikely to happen

His mother says he is **chasing rainbows** trying to be an Olympic athlete.

FRESH AS A DAISY

Meaning: To be full of energy and enthusiasm

After a good night's sleep, the child was **fresh as a daisy**.

Visit <u>www.LanguageLizard.com/Nature-Idioms</u> for additional resources for teaching and learning English idioms, including:

- English audio of this book
- Multicultural lesson plans for use in the classroom or at home
- Information on the origin of the idioms in this book
- Additional nature idioms with their meaning, usage, and origin
- Information on idiom translations and idioms in other languages

This book is part of the **Language Lizard Idiom Series**.

Visit **www.LanguageLizard.com** for a complete listing of the titles in this series and available languages.